DANGEROUS DRUGS

CRYSTAL METH

JEFF BURLINGAME

Cavendish
Square
New York

*To protect the privacy of sources, only first names were used throughout the book.
An asterisk (*) following a name indicates the use of a pseudonym.*

Published in 2014 by Cavendish Square Publishing, LLC
303 Park Avenue South, Suite 1247, New York, NY 10010

Copyright © 2014 by Cavendish Square Publishing, LLC

First Edition

YA 362.299
BUR

LIBRARY OF CONGRESS CATALOGING-IN-PUBLICATION DATA
Burlingame, Jeff.
Crystal meth / Jeff Burlingame.
p. cm. — (Dangerous drugs)
Includes bibliographical references and index.
Summary: "Provides comprehensive information on the dangers of crystal meth use"—Provided by publisher.
ISBN 978-1-60870-823-9 (hardover) ISBN 978-1-62712-059-3 (paperback)
ISBN 978-1-60870-829-1 (ebook)
1. Amphetamine abuse—Juvenile literature. 2. Amphetamines—Juvenile literature. I. Title.
RC568.A45B87 2013
616.86′4—dc23
2011023347

EDITOR: Christine Florie   ART DIRECTOR: Anahid Hamparian   SERIES DESIGNER: Kristen Branch

EXPERT READER: Russ Callaghan, PhD, research specialist, Social and Epidemiological Research Department, Centre for Addiction and Mental Health, Toronto, Canada

Photo research by Marybeth Kavanagh

Cover photo by Drug Enforcement Administration
The photographs in this book are used by permission and through the courtesy of: *Drug Enforcement Administration*: 1; *AP Photo*: 4; PRNewsFoto/Newsweek, 12; The Leaf-Chronicle/Greg Williamson, 45; *Newscom*: ZUMA Press, 6, 29; Multnomah County Sheriff/Splash, 9, 47; *Getty Images*: Visuals Unlimited, Inc./Science VU, 8; Mark Allen Johnson/ZUMA Press, 17; William F. Campbell/Time Life Pictures, 15; Jonathan Torgovnik, 27; Frederic J. Brown/AFP, 35; *SuperStock*: Prisma, 21, 25; Science Faction, 23; *Alamy*: Ace Stock Limited, 31; Paul Thompson, 37; Robert Holland, 40; Catchlight Visual Services, 55; *The Image Works*: Syracuse Newspapers/Stephen D. Cannerelli, 51; Jim West, 53 Most subjects in these photos are models.

Printed in the United States of America

CONTENTS

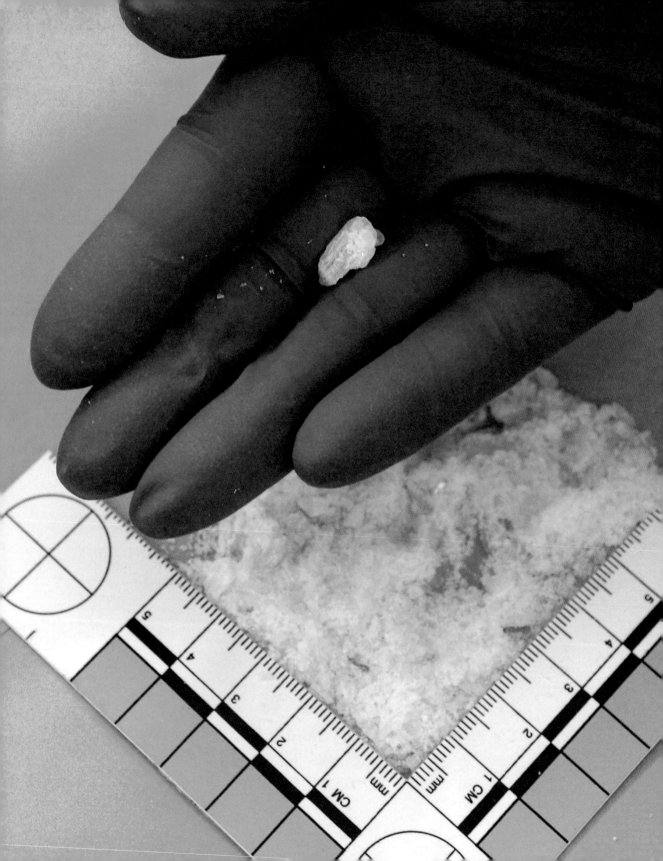

CHAPTER ONE

Easily Hooked

WOULD YOU EAT A CHEMICAL USED TO dissolve gunk from clogged sink drains? How about one farmers use as fertilizer or perhaps a metal used to make rechargeable batteries? Or does a combination of all three of the above items—with some cold medicine, paint thinner, and other poisonous and strange ingredients thrown in for good measure—sound even more enticing?

Despite the fact that all these items are labeled as dangerous, people do consume them, and they do so willingly. Specifically, they are consumed in the form of

Left: Crystal meth is a man-made drug that is very strong and highly addictive.

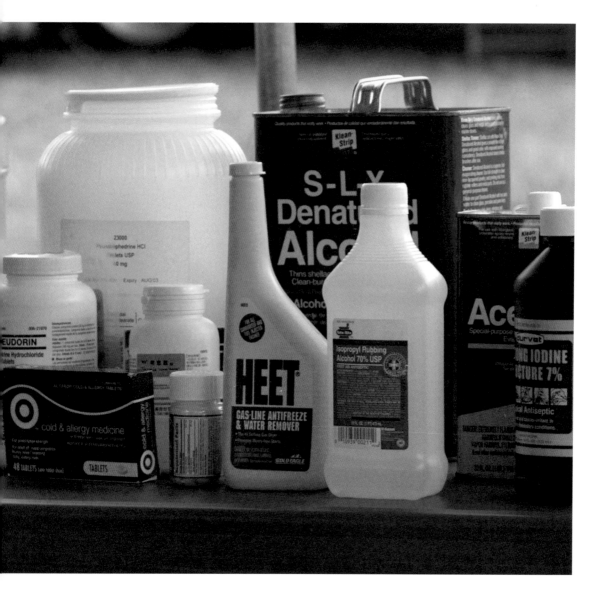

Crystal meth is a drug made from hazardous chemical products, as well as from over-the-counter cold medicine.

crystal methamphetamine, a highly addictive drug known for the mental and physical havoc it wreaks on those who take it. The drug, also known as crystal meth or crystal, is a **methamphetamine**, which is also known as meth. Both are types of **amphetamines**, drugs that stimulate the body's central nervous system.

The Basics of Crystal Meth

Crystal meth is created from the materials listed above, which are combined and heated, or "cooked," in makeshift laboratories in the United States and other countries. Crystal meth gets its name from its appearance: clear, chunky crystals. It can be smoked, swallowed, chopped up and snorted, or melted and injected into the body. The drug temporarily makes users feel more alert and energetic. They are able to stay awake for long periods of time. The drug triggers the brain's nerve cells to release large amounts of certain chemicals into the body, including **dopamine**, which is linked to feelings of pleasure, and **adrenaline**, which increases energy.

While the stimulating nature of the drug may sound inviting to someone who needs to finish a homework assignment or study for a test, any "benefit" of using

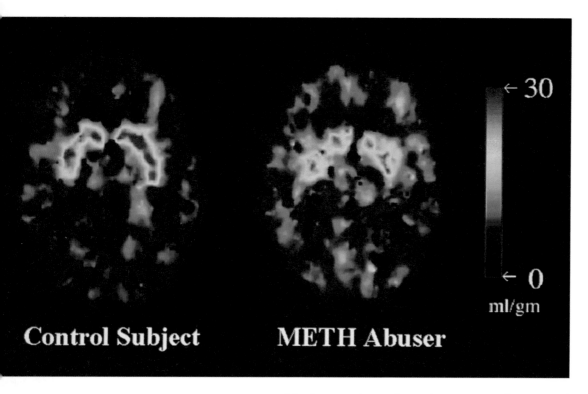

Control Subject   METH Abuser

A brain scan shows dopamine receptors in a normal brain (left) and in a meth user (right).

crystal meth is far outweighed by its negative effects. Users of crystal meth often act in violent ways and can be a danger to themselves as well as to others. After its effects wear off, users **crash** for long periods of time, sometimes days. Because of the persistent impact crystal meth has on the brain, longtime users can develop serious mental disorders. In addition, the drug suppresses the appetite.

Users often become thin and malnourished. Serious health risks connected to the use of crystal meth, in addition to brain damage, include organ damage, stroke, heart attack, tooth loss, and gum disease.

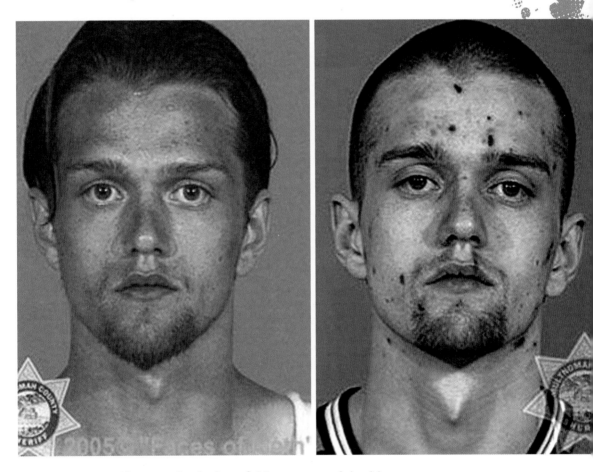

These two images illustrate the decline of this young man's health as a result of his crystal meth use.

Teens often get tricked into taking crystal meth simply because they are not sure exactly what it is they are taking. Some of meth's nicknames, such as "ice," "crystal," and "quartz," hardly sound like drug names.

STREET NAMES

Others—including "cheese," "Kool-Aid," and "sugar"—are also names of foods. Nevertheless, these nicknames and the ones in the following list all refer to crystal meth.

- amp
- candy
- cookies
- crank
- Debbie
- dirt
- gas
- ice cream
- Kryptonite
- rock
- ski
- tweak

The Numbers Don't Lie

Because the facts about crystal meth are known, it is hard to imagine anyone wanting to try the drug. It is especially puzzling that teenagers, who often spend hours fretting over the way they look, would use a drug that destroys the body and disfigures the face. Yet statistics show that teens as well as adults use meth. The 2009 National Survey on Drug Use and Health reported that 502,000 Americans aged twelve and older used some form of methamphetamine at least once during the month prior to the survey being taken. The 2009 Monitoring the Future survey conducted by the University of Michigan in Ann Arbor stated that almost three out of every one hundred tenth graders reported having tried meth at least once.

Ricky, a teenager from Spokane, Washington, told *Scholastic Choices* magazine how the drug nearly destroyed his life:

> No one has to tell me that I've changed. I know. All I have to do is look at the picture on my driver's license. That guy is 170 pounds. He's an A-student who loves his mom and his two sisters. He has a smiling, happy-go-lucky face.

PRO-CHOICE ON THE ROPES • CAN MOVIES SURVIVE?

newsweek.msnbc.com

Newsweek

August 8, 2005; $3.95

The Meth Epidemic

Inside America's New Drug Crisis

PHOTOGRAPH BY MARK ALLEN JOHNSON ZUMA

A methamphetamine user lights up

Newsweek magazine featured an examination of the meth epidemic in the United States.

12

I was that guy once. But after less than a year of smoking crystal meth, I weigh just 109 pounds. I look like a ghost, with sunken cheeks and little black holes for eyes. I haven't been to school in weeks. . . . My mother cries for me every night. I went to jail twice. I spent my days shoplifting or breaking into cars. I knew I was destroying the people who loved me. I just didn't care. I was hooked from my first hit.

Ricky's story is one of thousands of similar tales. In the latter half of the twentieth century, the popularity of crystal meth in the United States rose dramatically. Because it is relatively easy to produce, it became the drug of choice for many people who wanted to stay awake for long periods of time—for example, those who work long hours, such as businesspeople, doctors, and lawyers, as well as students, who used it to study.

At first, meth was imported from other countries, notably Mexico, but soon **meth labs** sprang up in rural areas in the United States. The abundance of such labs is the main reason why roughly 11 percent of eighth graders, roughly 13 percent of tenth graders, and a little more than 18 percent of twelfth graders say crystal meth would either be "fairly easy" or "easy" for them to get a hold of if they wanted to. While these numbers may sound upsetting given the dangerous nature of the drug, there was a time in the early to mid–1950s when methamphetamines were widely prescribed by doctors to treat a variety of maladies. Since those days, nonmedical meth use has steadily gained in popularity. In the 1990s it became a major problem, and government agencies focused their efforts on stopping the manufacture of the drug and placed restrictions on who could purchase the ingredients commonly used to make it.

An Aid to Soldiers

The creation of modern-day stimulants is generally said to have occurred in 1887, when a Romanian chemist named Lazăr Edeleanu created amphetamines in his laboratory in Berlin, Germany. In 1919 a Japanese chemist, Akira Ogata, created the more potent methamphetamine. It first became widely used by Americans in the 1940s, when doctors began prescribing meth for various illnesses, including asthma.

14

Police officers confiscated these bags of meth in a drug bust.

During World War II (1939–1945), American, German, and Japanese soldiers were given meth in pill form to fight fatigue and increase morale. However, the drug's benefits frequently were negated by the fact that many of the soldiers on meth became agitated and anxious and often were unable to get the rest they needed. In addition, many became addicted.

After the war, a drug closely related to meth, an amphetamine called Benzedrine, was widely prescribed by U.S. doctors to treat a number of health problems, including asthma, depression, and obesity. In 1967, for example, U.S. doctors wrote 31 million prescriptions for amphetamines. A majority of those prescriptions were given to women to treat weight problems and depression. When the advisability of such widespread use of amphetamines was challenged, the government placed restrictions on their use.

Reaching the Mainstream

Soon methamphetamine found its way to the general population. Common folk began producing the drug on their own. Some motorcycle clubs were known for manufacturing meth. In fact, one of meth's nicknames is

The contents of a raided Fresno, California, meth lab are laid out by the area's Meth Task Force.

"crank," named after a motorcycle's crankcase, where the drug was often stored. Initially, most meth manufacturing took place in California because of that state's proximity to Mexico, where meth ingredients were easy to obtain. Soon meth labs sprouted up countrywide, beginning with rural areas in the Midwest and Southeast. Because meth labs can be messy and smelly operations, they were usually located in isolated places so they would not be detected.

Today, a meth lab might be someone's home, tool shed, car, or even a hotel room. Meth labs are found in small towns and major metropolitan areas. This increase in manufacturing brought with it an increase in the availability of the drug. The number of users, many of whom are teens, also increased.

Because of the widespread use of crystal meth, being informed about how this drug works and what it does to those who use it can be helpful.

CHAPTER TWO

Health Hazards

THE SPEED AT WHICH CRYSTAL METH affects a person depends on how it enters the body. If it is smoked or injected, the effects are felt almost immediately. If it is snorted or swallowed, it takes anywhere from three to twenty minutes for a user to feel high. Once the crystal meth enters the bloodstream, there are a number of stages a user may go through:

> • *The initial rush*. During this stage, which can last up to thirty minutes, the drug has been carried through the blood into the nerve cells of the brain, where it causes heart

rate and **metabolism** to increase and blood pressure to rise.

• *The high*. Lasting from four to sixteen hours, this stage is one in which the user feels smart and confident and may become aggressive or argumentative. There is also an increased feeling of alertness and energy and a lack of hunger.

• *The binge*. As the high wears off (a period called the "coming down"), users often take more meth so that the high can continue. However, each subsequent dose is less effective than the previous one because the body develops a **tolerance** for the drug. Still, users often will continue taking the drug for several days, until they no longer feel any rush from it at all. During the binge, users often are hyperactive and hardly sleep or eat; as a result there is often weight loss.

• *Tweaking*. Occurring at the end of the binge, this stage is considered the most dangerous. The user may enter a psychotic state and experience **hallucinations**. Violence, both self- and

20

other-directed, and abuse of other drugs is common. Users also often experience intense itching, as if there were bugs crawling under the skin. In an attempt to relieve the itching, picking at the skin creates sores that can become infected and scar.

Hallucinations are a common side effect experienced by meth users.

- *The crash*. At this stage, the user's body is tired and worn out from lack of sleep and food and from general abuse, so it "crashes," and the user sleeps anywhere from one to three days.
- *Normalcy*. Often called a "meth hangover" or "return to normal," this stage typically lasts from two to fourteen days. During this period, the drug is out of the user's system, and his or her body is dehydrated, starved, and exhausted.
- *Withdrawal*. During this stage, which can last anywhere from thirty to ninety days, the user is depressed, lacks energy, and often feels suicidal. A craving for the drug develops. Most users, unable to cope with the challenge of quitting the drug and the challenge of life in general, turn once again to crystal meth, and the cycle starts over.

Serious Health Hazards

Crystal meth use has both short-term and long-term effects on the human body. Crystal meth is a **stimulant**—as is cocaine,

as well as the milder legal substances caffeine and nicotine. Crystal meth stimulates the body's central nervous system (CNS)—the part of the nervous system that consists of the brain and the spinal cord—which controls many of the body's functions. Overstimulation of the CNS can make a person anxious, irritable, paranoid, and restless. It can increase the body's temperature to such high levels that there is danger of convulsions or even death. Crystal meth use is also linked to anorexia, respiratory problems, irregular heartbeat, high blood pressure, heart attack, and stroke.

Chronic users who inject the substance into their arms with needles are at risk for collapsed veins, as well as heart-valve infections, pneumonia, tuberculosis, and liver and kidney disease. Perhaps the most severe effect suffered by long-term users is brain damage. Overdoses of crystal meth are common.

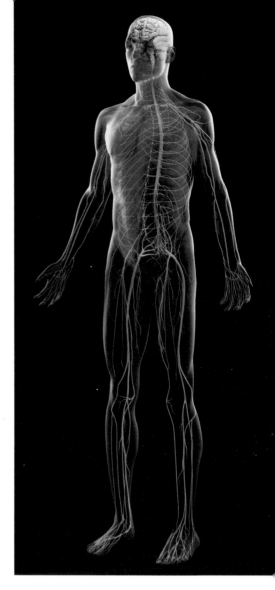

An illustration depicting the central nervous system. Crystal meth affects it in harmful ways.

One of society's biggest problems with crystal meth is that the drug does harm not only to the people using it.

Crystal meth users participate in risky behaviors such as unsafe sex and needle sharing that make them vulnerable to hepatitis, the **HIV** microorganism (which is responsible for AIDS), and other diseases that can be spread to others.

Those under the influence of meth are prone to sudden violent or delusional outbursts that can be harmful or fatal to people other than themselves. Cyrus Belt died as a result of such violence. Cyrus was only twenty-three months old when Matthew Higa grabbed the boy on January 17, 2008, and threw him off a bridge in Honolulu, Hawaii. Cyrus landed on a freeway, where a delivery truck ran over his body. A half hour before Cyrus died, he had been found sitting in the middle of a street by a police officer. He then was handed over to Higa, his mother's boyfriend. Higa, who had smoked crystal meth earlier in the day, admitted to being semiconscious when he committed the crime. Cyrus's mother was smoking crystal meth at a gambling parlor at the time of the boy's death.

Higa eventually was sentenced to life in prison. The prosecutor in the case, Peter Carlisle, said of crystal meth, "It destroyed the lives of everybody who was surrounding the child. And now it's destroyed the defendant's life as well."

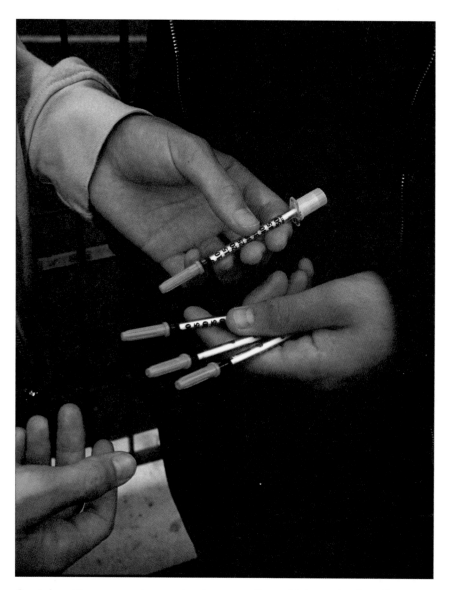

Crystal meth users are known to share needles, which can lead to diseases such as AIDS and hepatitis.

A Deadly Process

Even the process of manufacturing crystal meth can harm or kill. Those making the drug illegally oftentimes do not know enough about what they are doing. They may not know exactly how much of an ingredient to add to a mix or how hot to heat the meth when they cook it. They may not be aware of the dangerous reactions that can occur when certain chemicals are mixed together. They may breathe in the toxic fumes created during the cooking process or be careless in other ways.

Many illegal meth labs have exploded and severely burned or killed their occupants. The toxins released into the air in such explosions are harmful. Even when there is no explosion, the fumes produced in makeshift labs, such as those set up in hotel rooms and in rooms in private homes, can be a danger to anyone staying in them even after the process is completed. The fumes can kill quickly by stopping the heart or by suffocation or slowly, by causing permanent nerve, brain, or kidney damage.

Meth use can also be hazardous to the environment. Users often dump their leftover cooking materials wherever they can. Those materials poison the soil and eventually enter the local water supply.

This young man was severely burned when the meth lab he was running exploded.

Crystal meth is used by people of all ages and socio-economic statuses. Today, men and women use it in almost equal numbers. Crystal meth sometimes is used recreationally at **rave parties**, typically attended by teens and young adults. As mentioned earlier, students use it as a study aid or to help lose weight. There is no one type of person more likely to use meth than any other.

CHAPTER THREE

Meth's Ugly Faces

THE FACES OF THOSE ADDICTED TO crystal meth are not pretty sights. They often are sunken in and covered with boils, scabs, and open wounds. Many times, a user's teeth have fallen victim to **meth mouth**, a common malady suffered by habitual users. It is also common for those who use meth to suffer from dry mouth; that is, a lack of saliva, a secretion in the mouth that normally protects teeth against acidic foods and other substances. Without saliva, bacteria in the mouth build up, and the resulting acidic environment destroys the teeth.

Teen meth users in particular drink sugary sodas to try to "fix" their dry mouth. They also clench and grind their teeth when they are in an anxious state. Combine these factors with overall poor dental hygiene, and various levels of tooth decay occur rather quickly in crystal meth users. Sometimes the teeth crack and decay but remain intact. In severe cases, teeth may fall out. The gums of users often are infected and diseased, as well.

Experts are trying to figure out why some meth users are able to escape meth mouth altogether while others are afflicted with it relatively quickly. What they do know is that meth mouth is not pretty. "What I can tell you is what I have seen," said Stephen Wagner, a dentist in Albuquerque, New Mexico. "It looks like someone has taken a hammer to these teeth and shattered them." An Arizona dentist named Eric Curtis said that in his practice,

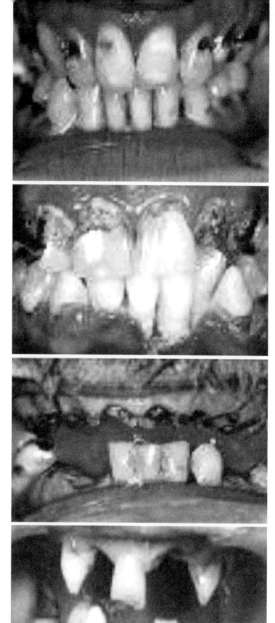

These photos are examples of extreme tooth decay resulting from crystal meth abuse.

he mostly sees meth mouth in teenagers. Even if he is able fix the damage, it will return if the patients do not stop using.

Odd as it may sound, one does not even need to be a meth user to suffer meth mouth. In April 2011 a mother from La Porte, Indiana, was given prison time for neglecting her six-year-old daughter after the child was found to have meth mouth from being exposed to the toxic vapors coming from a meth lab in her home. "To me, it's the worst of crimes," Judge Tom Alevizos said.

Impacts on Mental Health

The effects crystal meth has on users' mental health may not be as obvious as the physical effects of the drug, but they are there. Crystal meth and other amphetamines cause **anxiety**, **paranoia**, and **psychosis** in users. Long-term use can cause brain damage as a result of the high temperatures the body experiences when the drug is taken. Because of the damage to the brain's "wiring," the ability to think, speak, or feel is impaired.

Steve Wade suffered such damage. Five years after he overdosed on meth—and five years since he last took the drug—the thirty-one-year-old resident of Spokane,

Paranoia is one of the mental side effects experienced by meth users.

Washington, still props a heater against the inside of the bathroom door when he is in there. He fears that if he does not put up this barrier, someone will come in to get him. Ken Olsen, a reporter for the *Spokesman-Review* newspaper, wrote that Wade "shakes too much to shave with a razor. Some days, it seems the whole room spins. Other days, individual objects spin. Either way, Wade's always dizzy. He forgets key words in mid-sentence." Thanks to meth, Wade is permanently disabled and has to be cared for by his mother.

COLLATERAL DAMAGE

Crystal meth can be as devastating to the children of users as it is to those who are abusing the drug. A fifteen-year-old girl named Kai posted her story online at Kci.org, an anti-meth website.

My mother is a closet meth addict. . . . She has been using for about nine years now. I am almost positive she started using after my sister was born and her boyfriend went to prison. Since then it has been hell not understanding what was happening to my mom. She would stay in her room all day and leave me in charge of my sister. For years I had to take responsibility for the child while my mother unknowingly did her dope. I feared her back then because her moods were unbearable. She did things to me I will never forget in a crazy rage. . . . She constantly sucks all the money she can out of my grandma. When she will no longer give her money, she steals. And let me tell you this, she steals EVERYTHING. Every item in our house worth any amount of money turns up missing. Out of my room, the garage, my grandma's room, she even stole a pool table from our landlord getting us almost evicted. To cover up all this theft, she lies. She lies and lies and lies. There is no way to tell when she is speaking the truth anymore. I can tell when she's high, it is the only time she is pleasant and out of her room. If she is out of money when the high is over, she is literally a monster. She screams, abuses and says the worst things. She treats us kids and her mother like trash. She used to take her anger out on me as a little kid, but now that I am old enough to fight back she has stopped.... This woman is 34 years old, still living with her mother. She hasn't had a job for over a decade.... I can't do anything to stop her.... I have lost all the respect for my mom, and I have now lost all hope of her ever getting better. I am trying desperately to get away from it all. I hope to go to [Job Corps] soon or a boarding school, anything. I've never had a mother because of this worthless drug.

Getting Help

Breaking the cycle of crystal meth use is not easy, physically or mentally. Methamphetamine dependence is considered a chronic disorder, one with which relapse is common. Many drug counselors say meth users are their most difficult patients to treat. In part, the difficulty is due to the chemical changes to the brain that the drug causes, as well as to the fact that meth is highly addictive. Crystal meth treatment always begins with a period of **detoxification**, or detox, during which all traces of the drug are removed from the body. Detoxing usually takes place at a controlled facility where drugs are not present. Some detox facilities even use medications to help the addict cope with symptoms of withdrawal. The amount of time detox takes varies with each case.

According to MethNet, a website run by the Illinois attorney general's office, the best approach to fighting meth addiction, following detox, is **cognitive-behavioral therapy**, which teaches patients to think differently about the drug. Treatment also often involves the use of a twelve-step program, patterned after a similar program used for treating alcoholism. Each of the program's steps is intended to progressively pull the patients away from crystal meth and guide them toward living a drug-free life.

A drug rehab patient receives intravenous treatment for an illness brought on by withdrawal.

Regardless of how well early treatment sessions are going, many therapy patients will hit a "wall" somewhere between 45 and 120 days into treatment. At this time the patient often becomes depressed and experiences a strong craving for the drug as a means to combat this depression. For this reason and others, relapses are common. "Although recovering from meth addiction is challenging, it is not impossible," according to the MethNet site.

Methamphetamine treatment centers are busy places. Such is the case in the state of Missouri, which for years led the nation in meth lab seizures. The number of patients admitted to the state's publicly funded treatment centers has grown substantially over the past two decades. In 1993 only 146 admissions to these centers were related to meth use. In 2005 more than six thousand admissions were related to meth. By 2010 that number had declined to slightly less than five thousand—still an alarming number.

The sheer cost of treating crystal meth addiction can be prohibitive to those wanting help. **Inpatient** rehabilitation can cost anywhere from a few hundred to a thousand or more dollars per day; **outpatient** rehab costs significantly less but is still expensive. Health insurance often covers part or all the costs, but many variables come into play with treatment.

During the recovery process, some patients hit a roadblock and begin to experience depression and a strong craving for the drug.

Many users do not have insurance. For those people, if the state does not cover the costs, it is difficult to receive any help at all.

Life in a Rehab Center

Rehab centers generally are filled with well-intended, caring workers. However, for the patient, life is not easy in these places. For example, patients at the Visions Adolescent Treatment Center in Malibu, California, must undergo random drug testing throughout their stay; attend school three hours each day, five days a week; and take part in counseling groups. The teens are directed by teams of therapists, nurses, medical doctors, and psychiatrists. The facility is located in a rural setting behind a locked gate, and patients must stay there for a minimum of forty-five days. Families also must participate in each resident's recovery.

A basic goal of all crystal meth treatment facilities is to teach patients how to make new friends so that when they leave therapy, they will not go back with the crowd that got them into trouble in the first place.

CHAPTER FOUR

Paying the Price

CRYSTAL METH USERS COME FROM ALL walks of life. Truck drivers hoping to stay awake for long drives have been known to use it. So have business professionals looking to gain an advantage by working longer hours and people suffering from depression who want to experience the temporary euphoria crystal meth provides. The relatively cheap cost of meth, nicknamed the "poor man's cocaine," makes it appealing to cash-strapped adolescents.

Carol Falkowski, a researcher for the Hazelden Foundation in Minnesota, said, "I've talked to kids who've said

Some meth users experience a feeling of power and confidence in the early stages of abusing the drug.

it makes them feel like Superman. . . . When kids first start using it, it makes them feel so powerful that they can't see anything wrong with that, but this drug has the potential to ruin your life."

Writing on an anti-meth website, a teen named Rebecca said crystal meth did just that—it ruined her life. Rebecca said her troubled childhood—complete with an absent mother who abused the drug—led her to begin drinking alcohol and smoking marijuana at an early age. For her, those substances were **gateway drugs** for crystal meth, which she began taking when she was fifteen. One day, after running away from a rehab center in California, Rebecca said she went looking for some crystal and began prostituting her body to pay for her habit. She said, "I thought I had it all . . . I was using everyday and thought I just had it so good . . . [u]ntil that one night someone had pulled a knife on me, I was so scared . . . I gave him his money back . . . and after he left I called my dad crying. But I couldn't tell him where I was at, because I didn't want to be a 'snitch.' The pimp had told me if I ever snitch on him he would kill me and my family. If I could go back in time to never drink or do drugs, I would."

One Mother's Story

In January 1999 Vicki Kelly's seventeen-year-old son, Tommy, left the family home in the small town of Phoenix, Oregon, to hang out with a man who was a known meth user. The next day, Tommy and the man stopped by Kelly's home. Vicki knew something was up. "I realized Tommy was high on meth," she said, "and I knew you don't confront anyone in that state. I looked at Tommy and said, 'We'll talk later.' That was the last time I ever saw him—11:14 p.m.—the last minute I saw Tommy alive. I wish to God I had detained Tommy from walking out the door and done an intervention."

Details of exactly what happened after Tommy left home that night are sparse. For nearly a year and a half, Tommy's mother did not know much. She learned that the meth user Tommy had been with, Phillip Bendell, admitted injecting him with meth the night before he went missing. She learned that Tommy's older sister had known her brother had dabbled with meth before but that she believed him to be cleaned up until the day he left home. Kelly became an advocate for missing persons and helped get laws passed in her state to help those in situations similar to hers. She learned that when a loved

SPOTTING A USER

It is not always easy to spot a crystal meth user. If you have a school friend who is using the drug, chances are he or she will be trying to hide the fact. The signs to look for if you suspect a friend may be using include the following:

- missed classes or declining grades
- increased secrecy about possessions or activities
- mood swings
- new friends
- increase in borrowing money
- weight loss
- lack of sleep

one is missing, time stands still. "We measure time before and after Tommy disappeared," Kelly said.

In June 2000 police found Tommy's skull in a creek bed just outside town. The official cause of his death has never been determined, but his mother is certain meth played a major role. She has a message for anyone thinking about trying the drug: "Meth robs you of your soul and kills."

Solving the Problem

America's crystal meth problem has not been an easy one to solve because of the covert nature of many of the meth labs—and the everyday ingredients used to make the drug. The government moved to combat the manufacturing of meth, as well as other drugs, in 1970 with the passage of the Controlled Substances Act. In 1996 the Comprehensive Methamphetamine Control Act allowed police to confiscate chemicals used to make meth and also increased penalties for the possession of equipment used to make controlled substances and for trafficking in certain precursor chemicals.

In 1999 the Methamphetamine Anti-Proliferation Act, which amended the Controlled Substances Act, provided police resources and training to help combat meth production. The Illicit Drug Anti-Proliferation Act (2003) held accountable those who knowingly provided spaces for meth labs. The Combat Methamphetamine Epidemic Act (2005) limited access to cold medicines containing ephedrine and pseudoephedrine. All medicines containing those two chemicals were immediately placed behind store counters or in locked cabinets, which made them far more difficult to steal. The act increased the penalties for

A pharmacist at a national retail chain store places over-the-counter cold remedies behind the counter and out of the reach of customers.

those who sell any type of meth, including crystal, and for those who cook or deal meth in the presence of children. Laws were passed limiting the purchase of other chemicals, too, including certain fertilizers used on crops.

The penalties for meth-related crimes are stricter than they once were. Students caught with meth most likely will be kicked out of school and all related activities. Many companies require workers and potential workers to take drug tests, and those who fail them are either fired or denied employment in the first place. Legal punishments are stricter, too. Anyone caught in possession of crystal meth can be sentenced to up to a year in prison. Those caught selling anywhere from five to forty-nine grams of the drug face a mandatory penalty of five years in prison. If a sale results in a death or serious injury, the sentencing range is twenty years to life in prison. The penalties become harsher as the quantity of the drug or the number of offenses increases.

As they have for other drugs, educational programs have been created to help solve the crystal meth epidemic. Some of the programs have been created by the government, others by schools or private citizen groups. Anti-meth advertisements have become popular, as well. Some of those ads feature enlarged pictures of users with rotten teeth, sunken cheeks, and sore-covered faces and bodies. The Montana Meth Project has become well known for its graphic and straight-talking television, radio, magazine, online, and newspaper advertisements. The organization's thirty-second-long TV commercials depict scenes in which teens are abused, beaten, prostituted, or die, all from using meth. Its print ads feature graphic pictures with

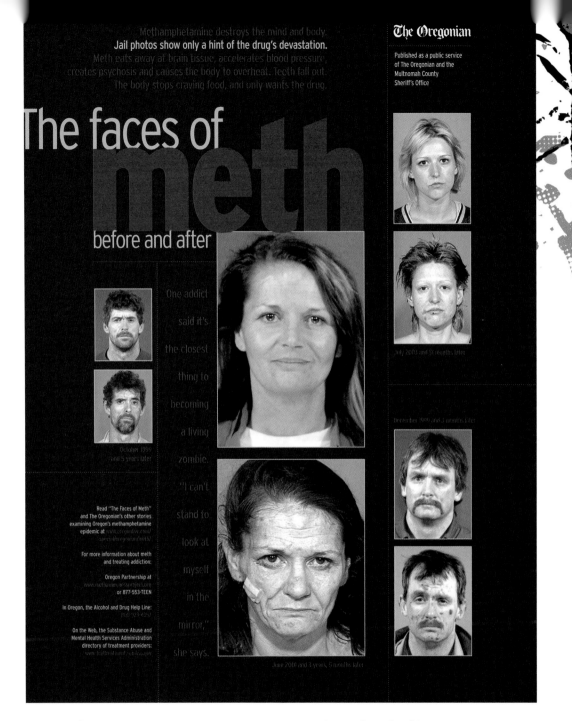

A Faces of Meth campaign poster shows the harsh realities of meth addiction.

messages such as "Picking for bugs under your skin isn't normal. But on meth it is" and "Beating an old man for money isn't normal. But on meth it is." The advertising campaigns have been judged successful.

Drug Courts

Society also has fought the war against crystal meth and other drugs by introducing a relatively new option for those prosecuting users—drug courts. A **drug court** is a special court that allows people facing criminal charges for drug-related crimes the option of entering a treatment facility rather than going to jail. The court provides the services deemed necessary to get offenders off drugs and keep them off. These courts also make sure people in their programs are tested frequently for drugs.

Those who make it through the drug court process often see the charges against them dropped or reduced. Those who do not complete the program face the threat of jail time. Today there are more than two thousand drug courts across the United States, and they appear to be working. Drug court participants are more than twice as likely to stay arrest- and drug-free than people who spent time in prison. Juvenile drug courts work almost the same as adult drug courts do.

48

WHAT TO SAY?

It can be difficult for teens to know what to do when they suspect or know friends may be using crystal meth or any other illegal drug. The National Youth Anti-Drug Media Campaign recommends following these four rules:

1. Remember that your friend's drug use is not your fault.
2. Never confront your friend when he or she is drunk or high.
3. If your friend becomes angry or violent, leave and bring up the subject later when he or she is calm. Or, you can refer your friend to a trusted adult if you are uncomfortable having the conversation.
4. If you are nervous about talking with your friend, recruit another friend who knows the situation to practice with you so that you can work out ahead of time what you are going to say.
5. Exactly *what* to say is another issue teens deal with. Suggestions include "I'm worried about you"; "You're using drugs to deal with your other problems"; "Your drug use is giving you a bad reputation"; and "I'm here to help."

These teens participated in an anti-meth awareness program in their school.

Saying No

Teens who are asked by their peers to try a drug often have a difficult time turning them down. They might wonder what people will think of them. This need for acceptance is a common issue teens face and is a tough one for many to overcome.

There are strategies to combat **peer pressure**. One of the best ways to avoid getting involved with crystal meth

or any other dangerous drug is to be prepared for the pressure. Practice strategies before such situations arise. Think of what you will say if you are offered a drug. You can say you are afraid you will lose your spot on an athletic team or your job. You can say you are afraid your parents will find out. Any reason not to use drugs is a good reason. No one should be afraid to say no.

The bottom line is that real friends will never pressure you to do anything you do not want to do. You may find that by standing up to peer pressure and saying no to drugs, you will become the "cool" one.

Have any of these tactics had an effect on the crystal meth problem? The numbers show they have. As stated earlier, in 2010 a little more than one out of every fifty eighth through twelfth graders said they had tried meth at least once. In 1999 that number was three times higher, with more than three out of every fifty students saying they had tried the drug. The number of those same students who said crystal meth would be "easy" or "fairly easy" to get also declined significantly during that time period. Crystal meth has not gone away, but it appears teens are getting wise to its ways.

CHAPTER FIVE

Making a Choice

LIFE IS ALL ABOUT CHOICES. GOOD choices can lead you to success; bad choices can lead you to despair. Taking crystal meth is never a good choice. While it is clear to most levelheaded teens that it is not smart to take such an addictive, poisonous, and potentially deadly substance, many still choose to take it.

However, most teens choose *not* to try crystal meth. Since the drug found its way to Middle America some two decades ago, awareness of the horrors the drug can cause has grown. Teen perception of the drug has changed appropriately. Today one out of every fifty teens in America has tried the drug at least once. Thus, in a school with one thousand students, twenty will have tried the drug.

While twenty is still too many, it is nowhere near a majority. It is important to remember that in society as a whole, crystal meth users are outcasts. So even if you find yourself in a situation where you are told "everyone is doing it," once you step out of that circle of peers, you will be in a larger circle where drug users are in the minority.

In addition to peer pressure, teens may turn to drugs out of boredom, as just "something to do." In such a case, the solution is to find something better to occupy your time. Staying busy can be a good way to stay off drugs.

Staying active and busy is a positive way to keep drugs out of your life.

Think of your friends who are not using meth. What are they doing with their time? Playing sports, singing in a choir, taking photographs, and journaling are popular hobbies you might enjoy. You might also consider getting a job or doing volunteer work. It is clear that there are many drug-free possibilities, and all are better than using drugs—even once.

Correcting a Mistake

There is no shame in having made a mistake, especially if you learn from it. You may be one of the teens who have tried crystal meth. If so, you need to understand that you are not trapped in a pattern and that you can break free of it. There are plenty of ways to get help.

The first thing to do is to discuss your problem with an adult you can trust. It can be a parent or another relative or a coach, doctor, or school counselor. If it is too difficult or embarrassing to discuss your situation with someone you know, there are plenty of resources you can contact where you can remain anonymous. A search on the Internet will turn up dozens of such places.

Oftentimes the decisions you make when you are young will seem silly when you look back on them years later.

Parents or other adults are ready and willing to help you and to discuss any problems you may have.

However, a decision to use crystal meth even once can lead to a lifetime of addiction, disease, sadness, and even death. When it comes to crystal meth, the best decision is to heed the advice of experts and to learn from the stories of those who have used the drug. The best decision is not to give crystal meth an opportunity to control your body and your mind.

Glossary

adrenaline a hormone secreted by the body that increases the heart rate and raises blood pressure

amphetamine a drug that stimulates the central nervous system

anxiety mental distress; a feeling of worry, nervousness, or unease

cognitive-behavioral therapy a type of talk therapy used by counselors to help patients become aware of and change patterns of thinking that can lead to such conditions as depression and anxiety

crash to experience exhaustion following a prolonged episode of drug use

detoxification treatment meant to rid the body of alcohol or other drugs

dopamine a chemical in the central nervous system that affects the brain's reward and pleasure systems

drug court a special court that handles cases involving substance abuse

gateway drug a drug, such as alcohol or marijuana, that is believed to lead to the use of more addictive drugs

hallucination a sensory experience of something that does not exist outside the mind

HIV the human immunodeficiency virus, which causes acquired immune deficiency syndrome (AIDS)

inpatient relating to a patient of a hospital or treatment facility who receives lodging and food as well as treatment

metabolism the group of processes by which substances in the cells of living things are broken down or built up

methamphetamine also called meth; an addictive stimulant from the amphetamine family that affects the central nervous system when ingested

meth lab any room or building in which methamphetamine is produced

meth mouth heavy tooth decay that is often a by-product of methamphetamine use

outpatient relating to a patient who receives treatment at a hospital or treatment facility but does not stay overnight

paranoia a mental disorder characterized by intense fear or suspicion that is frequently not based in reality

peer pressure social pressure from those someone associates with

psychosis a severe mental disorder that often includes hallucinations and paranoia

rave party a type of dance party frequented by teens and young adults that features fast music and flashing lights

stimulant a substance that raises the body's level of physiological activity

tolerance the ability to adjust to food or drugs so that their effects are experienced less strongly

Find Out More

Books

Etinghoff, Kim. *Methamphetamine: Unsafe Speed.* Broomall, PA: Mason Crest, 2008.

Landau, Elaine. *Meth: America's Drug Epidemic.* Minneapolis, MN: Twenty-First Century Books, 2008.

Marshall Cavendish Reference. *Drugs of Abuse.* New York: Marshall Cavendish, 2012.

Marshall Cavendish Reference. *Substance Abuse, Addiction, and Treatment.* New York: Marshall Cavendish, 2012.

DVDs

America's Crystal Meth Epidemic. A&E, 2007.

World's Most Dangerous Drug. National Geographic, 2007.

Websites

Enotah Anti-Drug Coalition

http://anti-meth.org/

> This site contains meth-related information and testimonials from users and former users, as well as a page of links on how to get help.

KCI: The Anti-Meth Site

www.kci.org

> This site includes dozens of crystal meth–related stories written by teens and adults, as well as articles and resources for teachers.

Montana Meth Project

www.montanameth.org/

The Montana Meth Project, Montana's largest advertiser, purports to reach 70 to 90 percent of the state's teens at least three times a week with its anti-meth advertisements. This site includes information on tolerance, psychosis, aggression, triggers, and cravings.

Say No to Meth

http://saynotometh.com

The goal of this site is to teach young people the benefits and positive impact of saying no to meth and other drugs.

Index

Pages in **boldface** are illustrations.

About The Author

JEFF BURLINGAME is the author of several books, including *Alcohol* in the Dangerous Drugs series. His books have been honored by the New York Public Library, and in 2012 he won a NAACP Image Award. In 2011 he also received an Image Award nomination. He has won nearly a dozen awards from the Society of Professional Journalists, has been a featured author on A & E's *Biography* series, and has lectured at various writing workshops and libraries across the Pacific Northwest.